THE SECRET INGREDIENT
TO SUSTAINED RELATIONSHIP
AND POWER WITH GOD

The Wisdom in Humility

Nicholeen Williams

Trilogy Christian Publishers
A Wholly Owned Subsidiary of Trinity Broadcasting Network
2442 Michelle Drive
Tustin, CA 92780

Cover design by: Cornerstone Creative Solutions

For information, address Trilogy Christian Publishing
Rights Department, 2442 Michelle Drive, Tustin, Ca 92780.
Trilogy Christian Publishing/ TBN and colophon are trademarks of Trinity Broadcasting Network.

For information about special discounts for bulk purchases, please contact Trilogy Christian Publishing.

Manufactured in the United States of America

10 9 8 7 6 5 4 3 2 1

Library of Congress Cataloging-in-Publication Data is available.

ISBN 978-1-63769-354-4 (Print Book)
ISBN 978-1-63769-355-1 (ebook)

DEDICATION

To my husband Christopher and daughter Jhenelle for their consistent support in this book writing venture! Also, to my Mother, my longest standing supporter!

CONTENTS

CONTENTS

FOREWORD

There is an innate connection between the designer and his design, the creature, and the Creator. While with the inanimate, the design only moves with the touch of the designer, the bond between the creature and the Creator impels them to actively pursue relationship that produces mutual interaction. We are created in the image and likeness of God with limitless potential to subdue, replenish, and have dominion. Embracing that mandate from the Book of beginnings, we are reassured by the embodiment of God in Christ Jesus, that with His ascension, we now have the capacity to do "greater works" than we have seen. In our quest to live according to our God assigned purpose and become all that we are created to be, relationship with our Creator becomes paramount in that pursuit. In this book, we are presented with the secret ingredient to ensuring we can cultivate and sustain a relationship with God, our Designer, and tap into the power He has ordained us to access through Him.

Utilizing her experience of over twenty-one years in full time ministry; with over a decade of pastoral responsibility, including four years as Youth Pastor; Nicholeen Williams draws on her own sustained relationship with the Lord, her degree in psychology and a life as wife and mother, to present us with this simple, relatable, yet effective blueprint on sustaining a relationship with the Lord and accessing the power He has designed us to possess. Throughout the book, she weaves the theme like a tapestry taking the reader on this insightful journey using biblical lessons and principles, especially in Chapter 4, coupled with her personal lessons from lived experiences in Chapter 5.

The secret ingredient becomes evident once you are progressing through the book, however, it is the "how to" that makes the difference. Williams gives insight into "how to" cultivate this ingredient and sustain that relationship with God in Chapter 9. This practical approach not only edifies the reader but provides a guide to making it applicable to your life.

I met Nicholeen when we were both blessed to be recipients of USAID Scholarships to pursue Associate Degree studies back in 1993. She would go on to study at Broome Community College in New York, while I studied in Wisconsin. Over the years, I have seen her unbridled passion for the Lord and her willingness to sacrificially give herself to the building of His Kingdom. She is a lover of people and those that have worked with her in ministry and otherwise can testify of her genuine love and care. She is a woman of impeccable character with a firm hand but with the humble spirit of a good servant leader.

May the reading of this book bring you into deeper and more sustained relationship with your Creator and Lord and may the power He has ordained for you in Him become more evident with each passing day. Be blessed.

Pastor Stephen D. Ricketts
Certificate in Biblical Studies from the
Jamaica Apostolic Bible Institute
Chartered Accountant
MBA from the Manchester Business School in the UK
Bachelor's Degree in Management Studies and
Accounting from the University of the West Indies

PREFACE

To God be the Glory great things He continues to do!

In the year I got saved, January 1999, the Lord told me that I would be writing books. I laughed then as the whole thought seemed so farfetched, but, as I have been learning in the last twenty-two years that I have been walking with Him, His words will always come to pass.

I started writing this book in 2014 under the instruction of the Lord. I have started and stopped so many times. Although I was inconsistent, God exhibited much mercy and grace unto me. The personal testimonies in this book of my encounter with an angel and the Spirit of God spanned approximately seven years. As time progressed, I kept getting insight on this subject matter.

At the end of 2020, I felt a strong conviction that the Lord was about to pass the book to someone else due to my lack of diligence in completing it. He had already taught me on the topic of "Substitution." It was a horrible feeling in the pit of my stomach, and I petitioned Him for mercy and asked for the grace, drive, and tenacity to see the book to its completion in 2021. He granted me that request and then directed me to Trilogy Publishers that I never even knew existed and opened the door for a great partnership.

This is the Lord's doing, and it is marvelous in my eyes!

Family

ACKNOWLEDGMENTS

To my Beloved husband, daughter and mother to whom this book is dedicated, thanks for your love, patience, encouragement and boost.

To my Sanctuary of Love and Restoration (SOLAR) Family for their continued support and push. Truly you have been such an inspiration. I am glad God gave us each other.

Petrena Cato, thanks for that extra push in the start of what I believe will have a ripple effect in my forward movement in the Kingdom of the living God.

To my mentee, Doneilia, for being such a great cheerleader and prayer partner.

To the early morning prayer group and mentee Javan, thanks a million for the continued coverage in prayer.

To those that helped to finance this book, my mother Sybil Bell, Uncle Vincent, and his wife Ruther Miller, and the NLCCI City of Hope Family.

To the Linton family, Pastor Pete, Charmaine, and Nicholas for the encouragement to pursue what God laid on my heart to do.

To Trilogy and Pastor Stephanie Thomas for the delicate handling of this book.

INTRODUCTION

When the Lord dropped it in my heart to teach on humility at our church, I was told to do this as it was a pre-requisite to Him fulfilling His word of "Fame and Fortune in the midst of Famine" that we got at our watch night service when we were crossing over into 2014. It has always been God's desire for us to know how to maintain our gain and so we had to learn wisdom and humility so that when the abundance comes, it will not take wings and fly through inappropriate handling of blessings, promotions, and increase.

For years I have been an observer of many men and women of God. This interest of humility, however, was first sparked when I became an Armour Bearer for my father in the Gospel, Pastor Andrew Steele, which opened several opportunities to closely serve great preachers and teachers from Jamaica and around the world. I have served the immensely proud and watched their lives, as well as the very humble. Over the years, those that were very humble were the most impactful for me. They possessed something about them that pushed me to God, and not pull me to themselves or their apparent accomplishments and possessions.

This book contains a composite of research from online sources, from the book *Final Quest* by Rick Joyner, my personal experiences and revelations and lessons from the Word of God.

It is my prayer that through this book, an understanding of the power and wisdom that lies in humility will be grasped and pursued in the name of Jesus! It is one of the secret ingredients to a sustained relationship and power with God!

WHAT IS HUMILITY?

Dictionary Definitions

[1] Humility

The quality or condition of being humble; modest opinion or estimate of one's own importance, rank, etc. meekness.

[2]Humble

1. conscious of one's failings.
2. unpretentious; lowly:
3. deferential or servile
4. not proud or arrogant; modest: *to be humble although successful.*
5. having a feeling of insignificance, inferiority, subservience, etc.:

---

[1] "Humility," in *Dictionary.com* (Lexico LLC, n.d.)
[2] "Humble," in *Dictionary.com* (Lexico LLC, n.d.)

6. low in rank, importance, status, quality, etc.; lowly: *of humble origin;*
7. courteously respectful: *In my humble opinion you are wrong.*
8. low in height, level, etc.; small in size:

Biblical definitions

[3]Strong's Exhaustive Concordance

HEBREW

Anavah (an-aw-vaw')
condescension, human and subjective (modesty), or divine and objective (clemency)—gentleness, humility, meekness.

This is used in the scriptures below:

Proverbs 15:33 (KJV)

> *The fear of the Lord is the instruction of wisdom; and before honour is humility.*

---

[3] (Biblehub.com 2004-2021)

Proverbs 18:12 (KJV)

> *Before destruction, the heart of
> man is haughty, and before hon-
> our is humility.*

Proverbs 22:4 (KJV)

> *By humility and the fear of the
> Lord are riches, and honour, and
> life.*

Scriptures:

Deuteronomy 8:3 (KJV)

> *And He humbled thee, and suf-*
> *fered thee to hunger, and fed thee*
> *with manna, which thou knewest*
> *not, neither did thy fathers know;*
> *that He might make thee know*
> *that man doth not live by bread*
> *only, but by every word that pro-*
> *ceedeth out of the mouth of the*
> *Lord doth man live.*

[4]Humbled—Hebrew—`anah (aw-naw')

Strong's Concordance

anah: to be bowed down or afflicted, to depress.

Colossians 2:18 (KJV)

> *Let no man beguile you of your*
> *reward in a voluntary humil-*
> *ity and worshipping of angels,*
> *intruding into those things which*

---

[4] (Biblehub.com 2004-2021)

*he hath not seen, vainly puffed
up by his fleshly mind,*

[5]KJV Lexicon Greek

Tapeinophrosune[5] tap-i-nof-ros-oo'-nay: humiliation of mind, i.e. modesty—humbleness of mind, humility (of mind, loneliness (of mind).

So, in essence, humility can be seen as a virtue that one can have naturally or cultivate, that will cause the individual to have a balanced opinion of themself, be courteously respectful, have the heart of a servant and a consciousness of one's failings, but is not hindered by them. It has a lot to do with our way of thinking as well. (*For as he thinks in his heart, so is he...* Proverbs 23:7, KJV.) In depressing oneself, it means not to put such a high price tag on yourself in comparison to the price or value you place on others.

Someone who has a balanced opinion of themself is aware of who they are, their capabilities, strengths and weaknesses and is not hindered or motivated by either. They tend to be more purpose driven.

---

[5] (Biblehub.com 2004-20021)

WHAT HUMILITY IS NOT

It is not equal to low self-esteem by any stretch of the imagination. An individual with low self-esteem does not think much of themself or believe they have much to offer, that they are failures in comparison to others. They often find themselves unattractive and believe that this is the opinion of all those that look at them. They have a hard time accepting that God has made them beautiful, that when He made man, He said, *"VERY GOOD!"* This therefore cannot be equated to humility since it is not having a balanced opinion of oneself. Having a balanced opinion of oneself means one does not think too high or too low of themself. They do not esteem themselves more highly than they ought to think. Also, since they are aware of their own failings, usually causes them to be patient, and more understanding of the human nature and its frailties and are not easily offended. Someone with the virtue of humility is usually great at helping others toward restoration and reconciliation.

Insecurity is not humility either, as persons that are insecure tend to doubt themselves and are not confident in their abilities and are often unstable emotionally. Persons that are insecure often require constant validation and when validation is absent, they may compensate through arrogance, develop compulsions, or addictions.

I was once in a relationship in which I was rather insecure. In retrospect, I recognize that it was hard on the person as I was always seeking approval and commendations for the things that I did. For that person, it was tiring and draining and sucked the life and fun out of the relationship. Thank God for a renewed mind!

Being quiet or reserved is not being humble either! Not speaking up or standing up for your rights is not humility in most cases either. Christ is one of the ultimate examples of humility, yet He got upset, turned over the tables, cast the thieves out of the sacred temple and rebuked who needed to be rebuked. Even in this, He still was humble, He knew His authority and He knew His rights and He utilized that in a non-traditional way. We see where He was tender towards the woman that was caught in the act of adultery and the woman at the well, yet He was aggressive towards the religious sect. All this never changed the fact that He had a balanced opinion of Himself... He was still humble!

Humility is one of the more obvious character traits that help to distinguish a mature or maturing believer, as they would recognize that of a truth, there is nothing that they can boast about as though they were the only reason for the thing they invented, or for their skills or their health. The Apostle Paul asked the question in 1 Corinthians 4:7, KJV... *"For who maketh thee to differ from another? And what hast thou that thou didst not receive? Now if thou didst receive it, why dost thou glory, as if thou hadst not received it?"* Everything that we have, are, and have accomplished is by the allowance of God. Knowing this, it behooves us to humble ourselves under His Mighty hand!

Education/Intellectualism, Spirituality or years in the kingdom are no indicators of humility.

Colossians 2 (AMP)

> *18 Let no one defraud you of your prize [your freedom in Christ and your salvation] by insisting on mock humility and the worship of angels, going into detail about visions [he claims] he has seen [to justify his authority], puffed up [in conceit] by his unspiritual mind, 19 and not holding fast to the head [of the body, Jesus Christ], from whom the entire body, supplied*

*and knit together by its joints and
ligaments, grows with the growth
[that can come only] from God.[20]
If you have died with Christ to
the [i]elementary principles of
the world, why, as if you were
still living in the world, do you
submit to rules and regulations,
such as, [21] "Do not handle [this],
do not taste [that], do not [even]
touch!"? [22] (these things all perish
with use)—in accordance with the
commandments and teachings of
men. [23] These practices indeed
have the appearance [that popularly passes as that] of wisdom
in self-made religion and mock
humility and severe treatment of
the body (asceticism) but are of no
value against sinful indulgence
[because they do not honor God].*

In the body of Christ these days there is
just a lot of madness it seems. I have never seen
the emergence of so many prophets, pastors
and teachers all claiming to have frequent vis-
itations from God so therefore we must believe
them. I personally have been bit by enough of

these persons to be on guard and to learn to filter people and their messages through the Spirit of God and the Word of God. In instances where I am not sure, I leave it alone and do not simply jump on board. We are certainly in the last days, so the adversary has turned up his game. The adversary is aware of the power of a humble person and the impact it has on God when He sees humility. The devil is therefore bent on lulling people into a false sense of security that they are humble, or that the ministry they are attached to is led by someone who is humble in nature. The Spirit of humility in and of itself is very calming, reassuring and often offers hope in the midst of what seems hopeless.

The Saints at Colossae were encouraged to not pay attention to what persons who were exalting themselves had to say, but to keep the focus on Christ our Mediator, our High Priest and Intercessor. We are to give reverence and respect to leadership but not worship. Several of these men and women of God have not recognized that by virtue of their lifestyles, practices, and teachings they are encouraging people to idolize them. Whenever the Apostle Paul sensed that persons were giving to him more than that which was due, he corrected them. In Acts 14:1-16, KJV where an account was given of people wanting to worship Paul and Barnabas because of a miracle that was done through them, they tore their clothes and spoke strongly against this action. Some of these leaders love so much the praises of men that they continue to heap it up on themselves and then find themselves in error.

A close acquaintance of mine has a relative that became impressed by a particular prophetess and sought to get close to her. The person did, and from that closeness developed the individual changed in many disappointing ways. They pumped so much into this prophetess according to instructions the prophetess said she got from the Lord, that. that relative lost a lot of things and became very poor. She is still clinging to the prophetess and the prophetess is still demanding that she sacrifice. When humility is at work in an individual, compassion and care for humanity is also at work. A humble person cares for the welfare and advancement of others, just as they do for themselves!

There was a time I armour bore, this man of God that was a prophet. He had some peculiar requests. He would instruct all of us that were assigned to serve him that we should never be higher than him. What this meant is that, if he was standing, we would sit and if he was sitting, we would have to kneel. We could only speak if we were directly addressed as outside of that we were chided for becoming familiar with him. Out of respect to our Bishop, though we were uncomfortable with the request we submitted to his request. A few years later, this man was publicly corrected, and his name was in the media in his country. He had a few consistent years of hardship. When we suffer, it is to our greater benefit when it is for Christ's sake.

The scripture also addresses the outward showings of what people impose on others to say that they are walking in holiness or are close to God. None of these things are impressive to God. When the prophet Samuel was to anoint a king, who fit the bill based on external features was outrightly rejected by the God who searches man. It was at that point that the Lord indicated that He was a God that looked at the heart of man while humans looked at the outward appearances. (1 Samuel 16:7, KJV)

INSPIRING HUMILITY QUOTES

The following quotes further highlights what humility is and all resonate with me.

Humility is not thinking less of yourself,
its thinking of yourself less.
Rick Warren

It was pride that changed angels into devils,
its humility that makes men as angels.
Saint Augustine

Think not that humility is weakness;
it shall supply the marrow of strength
to thy bones. Stoop and conquer; bow
thyself and become invincible.
Charles Spurgeon

I believe the first test of a truly
great man is in his humility.
John Ruskin

*With pride, there are many curses. With
humility, there come many blessings.*
Ezra Taft Benson

Power is dangerous unless you have humility.
Richard J. Daley

Humility is attentive patience.
Simone Weil

THE IMPORTANCE OF HUMILITY

Philippians 2:5-11 (AMP)

*3 Do nothing from factional motives
[through contentiousness, strife,
selfishness, or for unworthy
ends] or prompted by conceit and
empty arrogance. Instead, in the
true spirit of humility (lowliness
of mind) let each regard the others as better than and superior
to himself [thinking more highly
of one another than you do of
yourselves].*

⁴ Let each of you esteem and look upon and be concerned for not [merely] his own interests, but also each for the interests of others.

⁵ Let this same attitude and purpose and [humble] mind be in you which was in Christ Jesus: [Let Him be your example in humility:]

⁶ Who, although being essentially one with God and in the form of God [b]possessing the fullness of the attributes which make God God], did not [c]think this equality with God was a thing to be eagerly grasped [d]or retained,

⁷ But stripped Himself [of all privileges and [e]rightful dignity], so as to assume the guise of a servant (slave), in that He became like men and was born a human being.

⁸ And after He had appeared in human form, He abased and

*humbled Himself [still further]
and carried His obedience to the
extreme of death, even the death
of the cross!*

*9 Therefore [because He stooped
so low] God has highly exalted
Him and has [i]freely bestowed on
Him the name that is above every
name,*

*10 That in (at) the name of Jesus
every knee [g]should (must) bow,
in heaven and on earth and under
the earth,*

*11 And every tongue [h]frankly and
openly] confess and acknowledge
that Jesus Christ is Lord, to the
glory of God the Father.*

O my! This scripture is so powerful! In this,
we, as followers of Christ, are being encouraged
to have the mind of Christ, to make Him be
our ultimate example of humility. Here it is the
humility definition of having a balanced opinion
of oneself is very evident. Though Christ was God
in flesh, God whom the universe cannot con-

tain, God who sits upon the circumference of the earth, God who heaven is His throne and earth His footstool, out of love for humanity, humbled Himself to be robed in a parade of human flesh. This great God restricted His vastness to come through the vessel of a young virgin just so that the lost, hopeless, and dying may live eternally! What a God! This is like a king opting to live the life of a pauper so He can teach the pauper how to survive and to get to the place of a king, by allowing himself to be touched on all points as a pauper! What a God! What a God Man!

He knew He was God in flesh, but never lauded it over us while He walked the face of the earth. In His humility He knew His assignment and that became His motivation. He knew who He was, what He could do, what and who He needed, and what He had to accomplish, these things kept Him levelheaded. He knew He was the second Adam and the implications of this. In Christ stooping so low, not just to become human but the cross experience, He was demonstrating very profoundly that in order to ascend, we first must descend; we must submit ourselves to God and His ordinances, recognizing our frailties and acknowledging His omnipotence, always remembering the cross and what it represented.

It is our motives that will be judged as actions and even words can be very deceptive. Having the spirit of humility will enable us to find it easier to be true to each other. When the woman was caught in the act of adultery and they all were gearing up for a stoning showdown, Christ spoke simply and brought to them a word of truth. This caused them to examine their own hearts and recognized that though their sin was not adultery, there *WAS* sin present in their own lives that made them just as guilty before a Holy God in whom there is no shadow of turning and no guile.

Therefore, humility is important simply because we are followers of Christ and Christ's entire life, from the non-traditional birth in a manger where His bed was in the feeding tray of the animals, wrapped in swaddling clothes, a simple childhood, a ministry that was despised by many that led them to betray Him and ultimately His crucifixion. Christ led an entire life of servitude, so we too must serve and serve well!

HUMILITY AS A GARMENT

1 Peter 5:5 (KJV)

> [5] *...and be clothed with humility: for God resisteth the proud, and giveth grace to the humble.*

1 Peter 5:5 (AMP)

> [5] *..., Clothe (apron) yourselves, all of you, with humility [as the garb of a servant,[b]so that its covering cannot possibly be stripped from you, with freedom from pride and arrogance] toward one another. For God sets Himself against the proud (the insolent, the overbearing, the disdainful, the presumptuous, the boastful)—[and He opposes, frustrates, and defeats*

them], but gives grace (favor, blessing) to the humble.

The Lord speaking through the Apostle Peter instructs us to clothe ourselves with the garment of humility. the following information was received from Biblehub.com:

> The Greek word for clothe from the [6]Strong's Concordance is *egkomboomai* which means to put on oneself (as a garment), to tie round in a knot.

> The same Greek word in Helps Word-Studies 1463 *egkombóomai* (from1722 /en, "*in* the condition" and *kombos*, "a roll, band, girth")—properly, the condition in which someone is secured (literally, "tucked up"); figuratively, clothed (securely girded).

> In Thayer's Greek Lexicon, STRONGS NT 1463 it states: ἐγκομβωμαι (from ἐν and κομβόω, to knot, tie, and this from κομβος,

---

6 (Biblehub.com 2004-2021)

knot, band (German Schleife),
by which two things are fastened together), to fasten or
gird on oneself; the ἐγκομβωμα
was the white scarf or apron
of slaves, which was fastened
to the girdle of the vest (ἐξωμίς),
and distinguished slaves from
freemen; hence, 1 Peter 5:5,τήν
ταπεινοφροσύνην ἐγκομβώσασθε, gird
yourselves with humility as your
servile garb (ἐγκομβωμα) i. e. by
putting on humility show your
subjection one to another.

Strong's Exhaustive Concordance: be clothed
with. Middle voice from en and komboo (to gird);
to engirdle oneself (for labor), i.e. Figuratively
(the apron as being a badge of servitude) to wear
(in token of mutual deference)—be clothed with.

© Copyright Mandy Barrow

Be clothed with humility.—In essence the phrase, be clothed with humility means to, "tie, roll, band, knot yourselves up in humility." It is to so tightly fit about us that it will not easily move by agitation or cause exposure by the winds of change. It was customary decades ago for slaves to wear aprons or "tie ups as a sign of their servanthood. So too should humility be about us that it becomes obvious to all that we are servants of the Most High God!!

In Rick Joyner's book the *Final Quest*, he spoke about a scenario that really pricked my spirit when I read it. He was recounting an experience he had in the spirit where the Lord was showing him a battle that was in array. (Rick Joyner, *The Final Quest* (Fort Mill, SC: MorningStar Publications, 2010), 50-53.

Excerpt

The Deadly Trap

"I then looked over the carnage below, and the slowly retreating demonic army. Behind me more of the glorious warriors were constantly taking their place on the mountain. I knew that we were now strong enough to attack and destroy what was left of this enemy horde. 'Not yet,' said wisdom. 'Look over here.' I looked in the direction in which he was pointing but had to shield my eyes from the glory emanating from my own armor to see anything. Then I caught a glimpse of some movement in a small valley.

I could not make out what I was seeing because the glory from my armor made it difficult to see into the darkness. I asked Wisdom if there was something that I could cover my armor with so I could see it. He then gave me a plain mantel to put on. 'What is this?' I inquired, a little insulted by its drabness. 'Humility,' said Wisdom. 'You will not be able to see very well without it.' Reluctantly I put it on and immediately I saw many things that I could not see before. I looked toward the valley and the movement I had seen. To my astonishment there was an entire division of the enemy horde that was waiting to ambush anyone who ventured from the mountain.

'What army is that?' I asked, 'and how did they escape the battle intact?'

'That is Pride,' explained Wisdom. 'That is the hardest enemy to see after you have been in the glory. Those who refuse to put on this cloak will suffer much at the hands of the most devious enemy.'

...None of them were wearing the cloaks of humility and they had not

*seen the enemy that was ready to
attack them from the rear.*

*I started to run out to stop them,
but Wisdom restrained me. 'You
cannot stop this,' he said. 'Only
the soldiers who wear this cloak
will recognize your authority.'*

In a next segment of the book, it spoke about
the power of pride, that it comes up from the
rear, cannot be seen and its arrows are not felt,
but the penetrated would simply feel the effects.
It would cause them to grow weak. Now they
would not acknowledge it and so they became so
weak, they could no longer hold up their shield
and sword, so they put them down. They started
taking off their armor saying they were no longer necessary. This positioned them for a spirit
of delusion to carry them away from the truth.

Many strong and powerful men and women
of God have been taken down by pride. The book
encouraged us to pay attention to 1 Corinthians
10:12, KJV:

1 Corinthians 10:12 (KJV)

*Wherefore let him that thinketh he
standeth take heed lest he fall.*

AMP

> *Therefore, let the one who thinks he stands firm [immune to temptation, being overconfident and self-righteous], take care that he does not fall [into sin and condemnation].*

The book went on to share that the mantle of humility is the highest rank in the kingdom although the mantle itself looks very plain and unattractive in the spirit. He was also told that heaven and hell have respect for those that wear this mantle and that no power in heaven or earth can stand against it. Rick Joyner said it was revealed to him that this is so because this is the mantle that Jesus Himself wore. God gives grace to the humble according to James 4:6, KJV and 1 Peter 5:5, KJV, so to be robed in humility is to be robed in grace, therefore the more we will reflect the characteristics, life and works of Jesus Christ Himself.

I shared this from Rick Joyner's book as the things that the Lord shared with me are confirmed and further explained in that book. For years I have said that the mark of a true believer that has a deep walk with God is their level of humility.

But I did not have this depth of information then. Pride can be subtle in its movement. It is like a creeper. It sneaks up on you and if you are not careful, you get consumed and not realize what has happened. I have seen pride attach itself to some persons of humble beginnings. For some, it is birthed through the mishandling of the praises of men. Others, it is a generational thing. Some, it comes when increases or promotions granted, and persons forget who permitted the increase. Some are simply specifically targeted by this spirit because of the position of influence they hold. The adversary knows how God responds to pride, and when persons of influence get caught up in pride it will spread or cause the humble to begin to suffer at the hand of the person infected by pride.

Jesus said in John 15:5, KJV, that without Him we can do nothing, 1 Timothy 6:7, KJV says we brought nothing into this world, and we cannot take anything when we exit. Deuteronomy 6:18, KJV says it is God that giveth us power to gain wealth. It is God that gives the breath of man according to Genesis 2:7, KJV, Ecclesiastes 12:7, KJV, says when we die our spirit goes back to God who gave it. If we are truly Bible believers, then we will remember that we are vessels that God can use in whatever way He pleases as all we have and hope to have will have to involve Him! I have said to persons to always remember that God at one point used a donkey to speak. So, for Him to choose us is a privilege and an honor and should never be seen as a right! If the body of Christ does not turn, there will be many more talking animals to report about!

Romans 9:21 (KJV)

> *Hath not the potter power over the clay, of the same lump to make one vessel unto honor, and another unto dishonour?*

St. John 13 (KJV)

Willingness, attitude, expectation.
Service coming from humility, and humility manifested in service.

> *[4] He riseth from supper and laid aside his garments; and took a towel, and girded himself.*
>
> *[5] After that he poureth water into a bason, and began to wash the disciples' feet, and to wipe them*

with the towel wherewith he was girded.

6 Then cometh he to Simon Peter: and Peter saith unto him, Lord, dost thou wash my feet?

7 Jesus answered and said unto him, What I do thou knowest not now; but thou shalt know hereafter.

8 Peter saith unto him, 'Thou shalt never wash my feet. Jesus answered him, If I wash thee not, thou hast no part with me.'

9 Simon Peter saith unto him, 'Lord, not my feet only, but also my hands and my head.'

10 Jesus saith to him, 'He that is washed needeth not save to wash his feet but is clean every whit: and ye are clean, but not all.'

11 For he knew who should betray him; therefore said he, 'Ye are not all clean.'

12 So after He had washed their feet, and had taken His garments, and was set down again, He said unto them, 'Know ye what I have done to you?

13 Ye call me Master and Lord: and ye say well; for so I am.

14 If I then, your Lord and Master, have washed your feet; ye also ought to wash one another's feet.

15 For I have given you an example, that ye should do as I have done to you.

16 Verily, verily, I say unto you, The servant is not greater than his lord; neither he that is sent greater than he that sent him.

17 If ye know these things, happy are ye if ye do them.'

Here in this Scripture the incarnate God girded Himself with an apron and washed His disciple's feet. This is some level of humility, as He had to physically get down to the lowest part of man to minister a cleansing! In those days they wore sandals through dusty and unpaved pathways. Therefore, the feet could get very dirty. It should also be noted that pedicures then were not common if at all, the way we know it in this century. Feet that are only accustomed to sandals can get crusty if great care is not taken to properly moisturize. So, to wash feet you had to not only get low but be prepared to deal with dirt and possible crustiness. To me, we should be willing to get ourselves dirty and go low to see to the cleansing of our brethren. We should be willing to stoop low to see to the restoring of our brethren when they are at the lowest point in their lives.

In Psalm 35:13-14, KJV..."[13] But as for me, when they were sick, my clothing was sackcloth: I humbled my soul with fasting; and my prayer returned into mine own bosom. [14] I behaved myself as though he had been my friend or brother: I bowed down heavily, as one that mourneth for his mother." We see where David on behalf of his friends went into deep intercession for their state to be altered. This is how we are to be willing to serve each other. We ought not to think that there is anything morally good that is beneath us when it comes to serving each other in the Kingdom. Galatians 6: 1-4, KJV, tells us that we should seek to see to the restoration of fallen brethren, it encourages the stronger to assist the weaker. But the attitude with which this is done is critical, meekness and humility is required. The Bible says if the right attitude in restoring is not done, then the restorer will fall prey to the same challenge that the one who is being restored fell into. We always have to consider our own frailties and humble ourselves before God in the way in which we treat with each other.

Humility

Lesson 1

Nebuchadnezzar—Daniel 4 (KJV)

> **4** *Nebuchadnezzar the king, unto all people, nations, and languages, that dwell in all the earth; Peace be multiplied unto you.*
>
> ² *I thought it good to shew the signs and wonders that the high God hath wrought toward me.*
>
> ³ *How great are his signs! and how mighty are his wonders! his kingdom is an everlasting kingdom, and his dominion is from generation to generation.*
>
> ⁴ *I Nebuchadnezzar was at rest in mine house, and flourishing in my palace:*
>
> ⁵ *I saw a dream which made me afraid, and the thoughts upon my*

bed and the visions of my head troubled me.

⁶ Therefore made I a decree to bring in all the wise men of Babylon before me, that they might make known unto me the interpretation of the dream.

⁷ Then came in the magicians, the astrologers, the Chaldeans, and the soothsayers: and I told the dream before them; but they did not make known unto me the interpretation thereof.

⁸ But at the last Daniel came in before me, whose name was Belteshazzar, according to the name of my God, and in whom is the spirit of the holy gods: and before him I told the dream, saying,

⁹ O Belteshazzar, master of the magicians, because I know that the spirit of the holy gods is in thee, and no secret troubleth thee,

tell me the visions of my dream that I have seen, and the interpretation thereof.

10 Thus were the visions of mine head in my bed; I saw, and behold a tree in the midst of the earth, and the height thereof was great.

11 The tree grew, and was strong, and the height thereof reached unto heaven, and the sight thereof to the end of all the earth:

12 The leaves thereof were fair, and the fruit thereof much, and in it was meat for all: the beasts of the field had shadow under it, and the fowls of the heaven dwelt in the boughs thereof, and all flesh was fed of it.

13 I saw in the visions of my head upon my bed, and, behold, a watcher and an holy one came down from heaven;

14 He cried aloud, and said thus, Hew down the tree, and cut off his branches, shake off his leaves, and scatter his fruit: let the beasts get away from under it, and the fowls from his branches:

15 Nevertheless leave the stump of his roots in the earth, even with a band of iron and brass, in the tender grass of the field; and let it be wet with the dew of heaven, and let his portion be with the beasts in the grass of the earth:

16 Let his heart be changed from man's, and let a beast's heart be given unto him; and let seven times pass over him.

17 This matter is by the decree of the watchers, and the demand by the word of the holy ones: to the intent that the living may know that the most High ruleth in the kingdom of men, and giveth it to whomsoever he will, and setteth up over it the basest of men.

[18] *This dream I king
Nebuchadnezzar have seen. Now
thou, O Belteshazzar, declare the
interpretation thereof, forasmuch
as all the wise men of my kingdom are not able to make known
unto me the interpretation: but
thou art able; for the spirit of the
holy gods is in thee.*

[19]*Then Daniel, whose name was
Belteshazzar, was astonied
for one hour, and his thoughts
troubled him. The king spake,
and said, Belteshazzar, let not
the dream, or the interpretation
thereof, trouble thee. Belteshazzar
answered and said, My lord, the
dream be to them that hate thee,
and the interpretation thereof to
thine enemies.*

[20] *The tree that thou sawest,
which grew, and was strong,
whose height reached unto the
heaven, and the sight thereof to
all the earth;*

²¹ *Whose leaves were fair, and the fruit thereof much, and in it was meat for all; under which the beasts of the field dwelt, and upon whose branches the fowls of the heaven had their habitation:*

²² *It is thou, O king, that art grown and become strong: for thy greatness is grown, and reacheth unto heaven, and thy dominion to the end of the earth.*

²³ *And whereas the king saw a watcher and an holy one coming down from heaven, and saying, Hew the tree down, and destroy it; yet leave the stump of the roots thereof in the earth, even with a band of iron and brass, in the tender grass of the field; and let it be wet with the dew of heaven, and let his portion be with the beasts of the field, till seven times pass over him;*

²⁴ *This is the interpretation, O king, and this is the decree of the*

*most High, which is come upon
my lord the king:*

*25 That they shall drive thee from
men, and thy dwelling shall be
with the beasts of the field, and
they shall make thee to eat grass
as oxen, and they shall wet thee
with the dew of heaven, and
seven times shall pass over thee,
till thou know that the most High
ruleth in the kingdom of men, and
giveth it to whomsoever he will.*

*26 And whereas they commanded
to leave the stump of the tree
roots; thy kingdom shall be sure
unto thee, after that thou shalt
have known that the heavens do
rule.*

*27 Wherefore, O king, let my
counsel be acceptable unto thee,
and break off thy sins by righ-
teousness, and thine iniquities
by shewing mercy to the poor;
if it may be a lengthening of thy
tranquillity.*

28 *All this came upon the king Nebuchadnezzar.*

29 *At the end of twelve months he walked in the palace of the kingdom of Babylon.*

30 *The king spake, and said, Is not this great Babylon, that I have built for the house of the kingdom by the might of my power, and for the honour of my majesty?*

31 *While the word was in the king's mouth, there fell a voice from heaven, saying, O king Nebuchadnezzar, to thee it is spoken; The kingdom is departed from thee.*

32 *And they shall drive thee from men, and thy dwelling shall be with the beasts of the field: they shall make thee to eat grass as oxen, and seven times shall pass over thee, until thou know that the most High ruleth in the kingdom*

of men, and giveth it to whomsoever he will.

33 The same hour was the thing
fulfilled upon Nebuchadnezzar:
and he was driven from men, and
did eat grass as oxen, and his
body was wet with the dew of
heaven, till his hairs were grown
like eagles' feathers, and his nails
like birds' claws.

34 And at the end of the days I
Nebuchadnezzar lifted up mine
eyes unto heaven, and mine
understanding returned unto me,
and I blessed the most High, and
I praised and honoured him that
liveth for ever, whose dominion
is an everlasting dominion, and
his kingdom is from generation to
generation:

35 And all the inhabitants of the
earth are reputed as nothing: and
he doeth according to his will in
the army of heaven, and among
the inhabitants of the earth: and

none can stay his hand, or say unto him, What doest thou?

36 At the same time my reason returned unto me; and for the glory of my kingdom, mine honour and brightness returned unto me; and my counsellors and my lords sought unto me; and I was established in my kingdom, and excellent majesty was added unto me.

37 Now I Nebuchadnezzar praise and extol and honour the King of heaven, all whose works are truth, and his ways judgment: and those that walk in pride he is able to abase.

[7]Nebuchadnezzar—"in the Babylonian orthography Nabu-kudur-uzur, which means "Nebo, protect the crown!" or the "frontiers." In an inscription he styles himself "Nebo's favourite." He was the greatest and most powerful of all the Babylonian kings."

---

[7] (Smith 2019)

HE REVELED IN HIS OWN ACCOMPLISHMENT

Could he have escaped Judgement? A resounding YES!

- ❑ He got twelve months in which to repent.
- ❑ He was told to break off his sins by being righteous.
- ❑ He was told to break off his iniquities by showing mercy to the poor.

This great King was shown much mercy by God. He was warned, never heeded warning and the penalty was meted out. He had to spend seven years living like an animal literally, when he could have learnt the same lesson as soon as the instructions were given. Lessons of humility I have learnt are the hardest to be learned, as God will go through drastic measures to ensure you learn not to be prideful. So many times, we insist on learning the hard way. Have Mercy O God! Pride stunts growth and /or causes regression. Just as how stagnant water has a stench, has many impurities in it and is often discolored, when we are prideful we become like stagnant water in the spirit.

Lesson 2

King Ahab—1 Kings 21 (KJV)

[18] *Arise, go down to meet Ahab king of Israel, which is in Samaria: behold, he is in the vineyard of Naboth, whither he is gone down to possess it.*

[19] *And thou shalt speak unto him, saying, 'Thus saith the LORD, Hast thou killed, and also taken possession? And thou shalt speak unto him, saying, Thus saith the LORD, In the place where dogs licked the blood of Naboth shall dogs lick thy blood, even thine.'*

[20] *And Ahab said to Elijah, 'Hast thou found me, O mine enemy? And he answered, I have found thee: because thou hast sold thyself to work evil in the sight of the LORD.*

[21] *Behold, I will bring evil upon thee, and will take away thy pos-*

terity, and will cut off from Ahab
him that pisseth against the wall,
and him that is shut up and left
in Israel,

²² And will make thine house like
the house of Jeroboam the son
of Nebat, and like the house of
Baasha the son of Ahijah, for the
provocation wherewith thou hast
provoked me to anger and made
Israel to sin.'

²³ And of Jezebel also spake the
LORD, saying, 'The dogs shall eat
Jezebel by the wall of Jezreel.

²⁴ Him that dieth of Ahab in the
city the dogs shall eat; and him
that dieth in the field shall the
fowls of the air eat.'

²⁵ But there was none like unto
Ahab, which did sell himself to
work wickedness in the sight of
the LORD, whom Jezebel his wife
stirred up.

²⁶ *And he did very abominably in following idols, according to all things as did the Amorites, whom the* L*ord* *cast out before the children of Israel.*

²⁷ *And it came to pass, when Ahab heard those words, that he rent his clothes, and put sackcloth upon his flesh, and fasted, and lay in sackcloth, and went softly.*

²⁸ *And the word of the* L*ord* *came to Elijah the Tishbite, saying,*

²⁹ *'Seest thou how Ahab humbleth himself before me? Because he humbleth himself before me, I will not bring the evil in his days: but in his son's days will I bring the evil upon his house.'*

King Ahab was an interesting character. 1 Kings 16:30, KJV stated that, "Ahab the son of Omri did evil in the sight of the Lord above all that were before him." This means he took evil to another level. He was an idolater and lead Israel into idolatry. To add insult to injury, he was married to a very wicked wife to whom he was very submissive. She knew how to "stir him up," (1 Kings 21:25, KJV).

In this account he had wanted a vineyard from Naboth and when he was denied he went home sulking and his wicked wife decided to have Naboth killed. God's anger rose up against him and His judgement delivered by the fiery prophet Elijah. However, the story took an interesting spin in that this wicked king humbled himself and threw himself upon the mercies of God. There is something about the aroma that comes from a humbled spirit that God is unable to deny or resist. Although God did not take back his judgement Ahab received pardon and the judgement was transferred to his son! This may seem unfair, but God knew that this evil that was in king Ahab was generational. He also foreknew the heart of Ahab's son that it would not be humble and so the judgment would still be justified. A humble spirit touches God in ways that nothing else does!

Lesson 3

Syrophoenician woman

Matthew 15:27 (KJV)

> *And she said, Truth, Lord: yet the*
> *dogs eat of the crumbs which fall*
> *from their masters' table.*

Mark 7:28 (KJV)

> *And she answered and said unto*
> *him, "Yes, Lord: yet the dogs*
> *under the table eat of the chil-*
> *dren's crumbs."*

This story has always marveled me in that here it is the King of Glory seemingly spoke down to this woman, yet she was unshaken because of her strong belief and persistent faith that the Man that she was talking to had what she needed. Therefore, she did not pay much attention to what was said but humbled herself. The result was that though she was disqualified from such kindness to be extended because she was not a legal heir, her request was still granted because of her humility and confident trust in the Savior.

How many of us would forfeit our blessings if the holder of the blessing were disrespectful or seemingly had a mean attitude? Look at how David humbled himself under Saul's harsh leadership and at no point was disrespectful. Humility is one of wisdom's offspring.

Several persons walk out of church because someone offended them. It makes you wonder where our priorities are, what is our main purpose for attending church. What are the principles that we use to give us the right to be disrespectful when corrected or when told the truth? If this woman had taken the bait of offense her daughter would still be grievously vexed with a devil. I wonder how many opportunities for change have we missed because we refuse to humble ourselves?

Psalm 119:165 (KJV)

> *Great peace have they which love thy law: and nothing shall offend them.*

Lesson 4

Gibeonites Joshua 9 (KJV)

³ *And when the inhabitants of Gibeon heard what Joshua had done unto Jericho and to Ai,*

⁴ *They did work wilily, and went and made as if they had been ambassadors, and took old sacks upon their asses, and wine bottles, old, and rent, and bound up;*

⁵ *And old shoes and clouted upon their feet, and old garments upon them; and all the bread of their provision was dry and mouldy.*

⁶ *And they went to Joshua unto the camp at Gilgal, and said unto him, and to the men of Israel, 'We be come from a far country: now therefore make ye a league with us.'*

⁷ *And the men of Israel said unto the Hivites, 'Peradventure ye*

dwell among us; and how shall we make a league with you?'

⁸ And they said unto Joshua, 'We are thy servants.' And Joshua said unto them, 'Who are ye? and from whence come ye?'

⁹ And they said unto him, 'From a very far country thy servants are come because of the name of the LORD thy God: for we have heard the fame of him, and all that he did in Egypt,

¹⁰ And all that he did to the two kings of the Amorites, that were beyond Jordan, to Sihon king of Heshbon, and to Og king of Bashan, which was at Ashtaroth.

¹¹ Wherefore our elders and all the inhabitants of our country spake to us, saying, 'Take victuals with you for the journey, and go to meet them, and say unto them, We are your servants: therefore now make ye a league with us.

12 This our bread we took hot for our provision out of our houses on the day we came forth to go unto you; but now, behold, it is dry, and it is mouldy:

13 And these bottles of wine, which we filled, were new; and behold, they be rent: and these our garments and our shoes are become old by reason of the very long journey.'

14 And the men took of their victuals and asked not counsel at the mouth of the LORD.

15 And Joshua made peace with them, and made a league with them, to let them live: and the princes of the congregation sware unto them.

16 And it came to pass at the end of three days after they had made a league with them, that they heard that they were their neighbours, and that they dwelt among them.

*17 And the children of Israel jour-
neyed, and came unto their cities
on the third day. Now their cities
were Gibeon, and Chephirah, and
Beeroth, and Kirjathjearim.*

*18 And the children of Israel smote
them not, because the princes of
the congregation had sworn unto
them by the LORD God of Israel.
And all the congregation mur-
mured against the princes.*

*19 But all the princes said unto all
the congregation, 'We have sworn
unto them by the LORD God of
Israel: now therefore we may not
touch them.*

*20 This we will do to them; we
will even let them live, lest wrath
be upon us, because of the oath
which we sware unto them.'*

*21 And the princes said unto them,
'Let them live; but let them be hewers of wood and drawers of water*

unto all the congregation; as the princes had promised them.'

[22] And Joshua called for them, and he spake unto them, saying, 'Wherefore have ye beguiled us, saying, We are very far from you; when ye dwell among us?'

[23] Now therefore ye are cursed, and there shall none of you be freed from being bondmen, and hewers of wood and drawers of water for the house of my God.

[24] And they answered Joshua, and said, 'Because it was certainly told thy servants, how that the LORD thy God commanded his servant Moses to give you all the land, and to destroy all the inhabitants of the land from before you, therefore we were sore afraid of our lives because of you and have done this thing.

[25] And now, behold, we are in thine hand: as it seemeth good

*and right unto thee to do unto us,
do.'*

*26 And so did he unto them and
delivered them out of the hand
of the children of Israel, that they
slew them not.*

*27 And Joshua made them that
day hewers of wood and drawers of water for the congregation,
and for the altar of the LORD, even
unto this day, in the place which
he should choose.*

Now the above story was very interesting to
me. The Gibeonites heard of the power and might
of Israel's God and were so afraid that they had
to come up with a con for their lives to be spared.
They were fully persuaded that a battle against
these people would have been futile because of
their God that kept giving them victories. The
children of Israel, under the leadership of Joshua
and the elders, were at a good place in that they
were walking in continuous victory.

Now the challenge was, that they were
so comfortable and confident that when the
Gibeonites came with their concocted story they

sought not the Lord's counsel. In verse seven one of the elders said, *"Peradventure ye dwell among us; and how shall we make a league with you?"* This verse indicated to me that their spirit was alerting them to the possibility of deception, but they did not pay attention. They went ahead and made a league with them, only to find out three days later that they dwelt among them. The leaders being men of their word that they swore by the Lord, could not dishonour what they said. But I really loved the attitude of the Gibeonites, they said we are in your hands, we will honour whatever judgement you meet out. I believe the level of humility shown by these Gibeonites opened up much opportunity for the anger that was stirred to be abated. God from that point on showed them kindness based on how He used them through history. From [8]Enduringword.com, below are the ways in which God integrated Gibeon and the Gibeonites into Israel's history:

- The Gibeonites became servants at the tabernacle, just as Joshua had commanded.
- Gibeon becomes a priestly city; the Ark of the Covenant stayed at Gibeon often

---

[8] (Guzik 2018)

in the days of David and Solomon (1
Chronicles 16:39-40 and 21:29, KJV).

- At least one of David's *mighty men* was a
  Gibeonite (1 Chronicles 12:4, KJV).
- God spoke to Solomon at Gibeon (1 Kings
  3:4, KJV).
- Gibeonites were among those who rebuilt
  the walls of Jerusalem with Nehemiah
  (Nehemiah 3:7 and 7:25, KJV).
- Prophets such as Hananiah the son of
  Azur came from Gibeon (Jeremiah 28:1,
  KJV).

These are examples of the great things God
can do with people who are sinners but come to
Him in humility.

Lesson 5

Rehoboam and the Princes of Israel

2 Chronicles 12:5-7 (KJV)

> *5 Then Shemaiah the prophet
> came to Rehoboam and the
> princes of Judah who had gath-
> ered at Jerusalem because of
> Shishak, and said to them, 'Thus*

says the Lord: You have forsaken Me, so I have abandoned you into the hands of Shishak.'

⁶ Then the princes of Israel and the king humbled themselves and said, 'The Lord is righteous.'

⁷ And when the Lord saw that they humbled themselves, the word of the Lord came to Shemaiah, saying, 'They have humbled themselves, so I will not destroy them, but I will grant them some deliverance; and My wrath shall not be poured out upon Jerusalem by the hand of Shishak.'

Rehoboam, Solomon's son had ascended the throne after his father walked in the ways of David for a number of years. However, after the kingdom was established and he was strengthened, he forsook the commands of the Lord. As a result, they were to be given over to Shishak the king of Egypt as their judgement. When they heard their sentence via the prophet Shemaiah, they humbled themselves and the judgement was somewhat reversed as He did not destroy them but gave them some deliverance. God, however, did allow things to be taken from the House of the Lord and they were their servants so as to be able to compare the harsh yoke of a foreign king in comparison to the easy yoke of the Merciful King of Kings!

Personal Experience

Based on my sanguine personality, I am a very sociable person. I love to have a good time and I have been told repeatedly that I have a personality that cannot hide even if I remained quiet. I got saved in 1999 and had to grow quickly as I was thrown into a leadership position soon after I started my walk. The first few years for me with the Lord was great but not so good with several persons. For a season I frequently experienced the power of the Holy Ghost where when I laid hands on persons as the Apostles did, they would receive the Holy Ghost. The Lord had given me insight into people's lives so I would be able to give a word of wisdom or word of knowledge. I used to fast very often but then I had a very discouraging experience, and I withdrew from the Lord spiritually but was still operating in the giftings. There were three distinct times in my first ten years where I had to be dramatically humbled by the Lord. For some it may seem embarrassing but, in my eyes, I simply see the love, mercy, patience and compassionate nature of God in operation, in that He never left me to my own devices which would have wrecked me, family, ministry and future.

My first experience was when I was praying a prayer that was like that of the Pharisee in Luke 18 and it was like I was watching myself and an angel showed up with a sword and placed it at my neck, I cried for mercy and began to repent immediately. I had to be delivered from a critical and self-righteous nature.

Luke 18 (KJV)

> *9 And he spake this parable unto certain which trusted in themselves that they were righteous, and despised others:*

> *10 'Two men went up into the temple to pray; the one a Pharisee, and the other a publican.*

> *11 The Pharisee stood and prayed thus with himself, God, I thank thee, that I am not as other men*

*are, extortioners, unjust, adulter-
ers, or even as this publican.*

[12] *I fast twice in the week, I give
tithes of all that I possess.*

[13] *And the publican, standing afar
off, would not lift up so much as
his eyes unto heaven, but smote
upon his breast, saying, God be
merciful to me a sinner.*

[14] *I tell you, this man went down to
his house justified rather than the
other: for every one that exalteth
himself shall be abased; and he
that humbleth himself shall be
exalted.'*

The next one was where I was on a spiritual
high where I would just look at persons and could
see their spirit and some of their deeds. One
morning in the heights of worship at church my
eyes fell on someone whom the Lord had revealed
something about them to me and in my heart I
said, 'look at her, as if she holy' and immediately
I was shoved to the ground flat on my face and
persons were thinking that it was the anoint-

ing, but it was no anointing, while on the floor I heard a booming voice saying, "Who made you Lord over God's heritage?" It was frightening and I had to cry out again for mercy again, repent, and humble myself.

The third experience was a warning and it never manifested, and I am trusting God that He will preserve me. I had a vision where it was that there would come a time where I would rise, and the people would put me on a pedestal, and I would begin to rely on my own abilities and gift-ings. I saw the pedestal rise high into the heav-ens and then out of nowhere an axe came from heaven and chopped the pedestal and I fell flat on my face. To this day, I have to pray that God will help me to keep the garment of humility about me that I will not exalt myself or allow anyone to exalt me above measure. I still pray that I will not pattern Lucifer in anyway by attempting to rob God of His Glory and I am trusting the cove-nant keeping God to preserve me and honor this request because I have asked. King Saul loved the applause of people more than the applause of God and as a result he lost his kingdom, his soul and caused his son to die prematurely.

Although it may seem as though my head is tough, we have to recognize that as humans if we don't keep some things ever before us, they will be forgotten. That is why in Deuteronomy 6, where the Shema is located, they are told to rehearse the fact that God is one Lord, in the morning in the evening, as the go, as they sit etc. It was important to God that Israel not follow the other idolatrous nations and remember that He is One! It is said by [9]George Barna a professor at a Christian University that, "Every twenty-one days, your people forget the vision," therefore, repetition in necessary most of the time.

So, God's words must be continually before us, so we do not forget and lose focus. It was only when Peter kept His eyes on Jesus that he was able to walk on water. We have to set our affections consistently on the things that are above to cause us to walk in alignment and agreement with the will of God.

---

[9] (Casey n.d.)

PRIDE A MAJOR ENEMY OF HUMILITY

[10]DEFINITION OF PRIDE

1. a high or inordinate opinion of one's own dignity, importance, merit, or superiority, whether as cherished in the mind or as displayed in bearing, conduct, etc.
2. the state or feeling of being <u>proud</u>.

The scriptures below speak of God's view on pride.

Proverbs 8:13 (KJV)

> *The fear of the Lord is to hate evil:*
> *pride, and arrogancy, and the evil*

---

[10] (Dictionary.com n.d.)

*way, and the froward mouth, do
I hate.*

Proverbs 13:10 (KJV)

*Only by pride cometh conten-
tion: but with the well advised is
wisdom.*

Proverbs 11:2 (KJV)

*When pride cometh, then com-
eth shame: but with the lowly is
wisdom.*

Proverbs 14:3 (KJV)

*In the mouth of the foolish is a rod
of pride: but the lips of the wise
shall preserve them.*

Proverbs 16:18 (KJV)

*Pride goeth before destruction,
and an haughty spirit before a
fall.*

Proverbs 18:12 (KJV)

Before destruction the heart of man is haughty, and before honour is humility.

2 Samuel 22:28 (KJV)

And the afflicted people thou wilt save: but thine eyes are upon the haughty, that thou mayest bring them down.

Job 41:1 & 34 (KJV)

Canst thou draw out leviathan with an hook? or his tongue with a cord which thou lettest down?

34 He beholdeth all high things: he is a king over all the children of pride.

Pride is something detestable to the Almighty. Lucifer was not the embodiment of pride when he was created. He was described as an anointed cherub. It is said popularly that he was the minister of music in heaven. The word says Lucifer tried to exalt himself above God. He was said to be beautiful and became blinded by his own brightness. Pride is so subtle at times and it often takes a discerning eye and ear to detect its presence. In Job 41, it says that Leviathan is king over all the children of pride. The description of this creature alone seems terrifying as it boasts of a creature that is given features that are strong, impenetrable and cannot be tamed or manipulated through human interventions. It is no wonder that when persons are under its control that they seem so impenetrable. People that have allowed pride to become a stronghold can identify it in everyone else but themselves.

STRONG HOLD OF PRIDE

A stronghold is a demonic fortress of thoughts housing evil spirits that:

(1) control, dictate, and influence your attitudes and behavior;

(2) oppress and discourage you;

(3) filter and color how you view or react to situations, circumstances, or people.

2 Corinthians 10:3-5(KJV)

> *³ For though we walk in the flesh, we do not war after the flesh:*

87

*⁴ (For the weapons of our warfare
are not carnal, but mighty through
God to the pulling down of strong
holds;)*

*⁵ Casting down imaginations, and
every high thing that exalteth
itself against the knowledge of
God, and bringing into captivity
every thought to the obedience of
Christ;*

To tear down this stronghold of pride, God's help will have to be solicited. A stronghold is known by the symptoms, which are characterized by behavioral traits. Once pride is detected or suspected, the individual has got to be diligent to repent of the actions that were associated with the necessary symptoms. They have got to renounce the connection and part with this strongman and ask God to replace it with right attitudes and seek to be girded with humility. I honestly prefer to humble myself as God's method of humbling can be very severe. But He can humble me any day as I must see His face!

Below is a list of the symptoms of pride majorly derived from the list in the book [11]*Demol-*

---

[11] (Dowgiewicz 2005)

ishing Strongholds. A description of each symptom is given along with the associated scriptures. How this list is used, is that you prayerfully assess yourself based on the description of symptoms and repent where necessary. As the individual identifies the symptom in themselves, they usually rate themselves from zero to ten. If there is a rating above zero repentance is necessary. When a stronghold is well fortified within an individual, they will find they have high scores for several of the symptoms. Now as I said, this must be prayerfully done as the strongman of this stronghold will try to convince the person that, that symptom is not present in the assessor's life. It is usually recommended that you get another assessment done by family members or friends that are closely related to you.

SYMPTOMS OF THE
STRONGHOLD OF PRIDE

- Haughtiness—blatantly and disdainfully proud: having or showing an attitude of superiority and contempt for people or things perceived to be inferior. (Isaiah 3:15-17, KJV)
- Ungrateful—Belief that you are entitled to anything you are given; failure to appreciate others; take others for granted (2 Timothy 3:2, KJV)

- Self-righteous—High opinion of your moral position compared to that of others (Luke 18:10-12, KJV)
- Self-centered—Obsessive egocentric pattern of thinking; "the world revolves around me" (Proverbs 21:4, KJV)
- Insensitive—Unaware of impact on others; a bull-in-a-china-shop (Proverbs 26:12, KJV)
- Materialistic—Obsessive desire to acquire and possess in order to gain recognition or prestige (1 John 2:15,16, AMPC & KJV)
- Seeks Positions—Viewing people and resources as means of fulfilling ego needs; relationships have little worth except to advance self; presumptuous (Proverbs 25:6,7, KJV)
- Stubborn—Such high regard for your own views that you ignore or denigrate the input and counsel of others (Jeremiah 7:24, KJV)
- Mocking—Belittling others through words or mannerism, disparaging their dignity (Proverbs 18:3, KJV)
- Vain—Conceit about your own importance, abilities, appearance, possessions (Romans 12:16, KJV)

- Spiritual Adultery—Perverting God's grace into permission to sin; serving "another spirit" apart from the God of the Bible (James 4:4-6, KJV)
- Impatient—Intolerant of delay or opposition; your time is more important than others (Ecclesiastes 7:8, KJV)
- Argumentative—Having always to have the last word, provoking, disagreeable (Proverbs 13:10, KJV)

HUMBLING EXPERIENCES ARE GOD'S TESTING TOOLS.

Deuteronomy 8 (AMPC)

> *2 And you shall [earnestly] remember all the way which the Lord your God led you these forty years in the wilderness, to humble you and to prove you, to know what was in your [mind and] heart, whether you would keep His commandments or not.*
>
> *3 And He humbled you and allowed you to hunger and fed*

*you with manna, which you did
not know nor did your fathers
know, that He might make you
recognize and personally know
that man does not live by bread
only, but man lives by every word
that proceeds out of the mouth of
the Lord.*

*⁴ Your clothing did not become old
upon you nor did your feet swell
these forty years.*

*⁵ Know also in your [minds and]
hearts that, as a man disciplines
and instructs his son, so the Lord
your God disciplines and instructs
you.*

In the above scripture, God humbled Israel
as a test of their substance and to prove to them
where their anchor should be and who the source
of all things really was! God humbles humanity to
remind them of His Sovereignty and their frailty.

HUMILITY AS A NATION

2 Chronicles 7:14 (KJV)

> *13 If I shut up heaven that there be no rain, or if I command the locusts to devour the land, or if I send pestilence among my people;*

> *14 If my people, which are called by my name, shall humble themselves, and pray, and seek my face, and turn from their wicked ways; then will I hear from heaven, and will forgive their sin, and will heal their land.*

This is a common scripture in Christendom. But it is one that is not properly understood. Here God gives a solution to those that are called by His name that are experiencing closed heavens or under afflictions because of God's judgements. It is my belief that this scripture is not merely from a national level but also personal. As individuals, we do sometimes experience closed heavens, periods where heaven is unresponsive to prayers and demands and commands.

There are also times when we are under certain judgements because of continuous unrepentant ways. So, whether it is a nation or an individual, the solution remains the same. In verse 14 He says, the first thing to set things in motion for restoration is that His people must humble themselves! This will open the door so the believer can set in motion that which is needed for repositioning before God and ultimately healing and restoration. Now humbling oneself in the Old Testament was often linked with fasting as it subdued the flesh that the spirit of the person can connect with the Spirit of God. See scriptures that highlight this:

Leviticus 16:29 (AMP)

> *[An Annual Atonement] "This shall be a permanent statute for you: in the seventh month (nearly October) on the tenth day of the month you shall humble yourselves [by fasting] and not do any work, whether the native-born or the stranger who lives temporarily among you;*

Leviticus 23:27 (AMP)

*"Also, the tenth day of this seventh
month is the Day of Atonement;
it shall be a holy convocation for
you, and you shall humble yourselves [by fasting] and present an
offering by fire to the LORD.*

Ezra 8:21 (AMPC)

*Then I proclaimed a fast there,
at the river Ahava, that we might
humble ourselves before our God
to seek from Him a straight and
right way for us, our little ones,
and all our possessions.*

Psalm 35:13 (KJV)

*But as for me, when they were
sick, my clothing was sackcloth:
I humbled my soul with fasting;
and my prayer returned into mine
own bosom.*

(AMP)

> *But as for me, when they were*
> *sick, my clothing was sack-*
> *cloth (mourning garment); I hum-*
> *bled my soul with fasting, And I*
> *prayed with my head bowed on*
> *my chest.*

Psalm 69:10 (AMPC)

> *When I wept and humbled myself*
> *with fasting, I was jeered at and*
> *humiliated;*

Isaiah 58:5 (AMPC)

> *Is such a fast as yours what I*
> *have chosen, a day for a man to*
> *humble himself with sorrow in*
> *his soul? [Is true fasting merely*
> *mechanical?] Is it only to bow*
> *down his head like a bulrush and*
> *to spread sackcloth and ashes*
> *under him [to indicate a condition*
> *of heart that he does not have]?*
> *Will you call this a fast and an*
> *acceptable day to the Lord?*

So, a sure way to solicit an open door in heaven is via humility which if an individual does not have can be cultivated. Fasting done the right way is a great strategy for this. Remember, Jesus returned full of the Power of the Spirit after His forty day fast! (Luke 4:14, KJV).

HUMILITY ON THE JOB

We have a saying in Jamaica "The humble calf sucks the most milk." What this translates to is that much more is made available to anyone that is of a humble nature. Therefore, humility does not only benefit Christians but also non-Christians.

I remember years ago working at a company where my supervisor was taking my ideas to the general manager and passing them off as his own. It was just before I became a Christian. He for a while kept communicating my ideas to the manager. I pretended not to be aware he was doing that. Life has a funny way of dealing with injustices. One day, he brought an idea to the boss that was questioned and when he could not clearly explain the idea, then he said I would be better to explain. His actions were finally exposed.

Out of that situation I got a promotion that was higher than his current post.

In this generation, the crab in a barrel mentality, meaning people believing that they have to pull people down that they can rise, is not the only way to rise. You can be assertive but not destructive to others. Remember that humility is having a balanced opinion of oneself so on the job you work hard and let the work be done with such excellence that it speaks loudly of who you are. Excellence tends to shine like a star, and it does not matter what anyone does it cannot stay hidden for long.

In our work places our employer is like a god, in terms of authority. We are expected to respect and to obey and be compensated. When we work well and are humble, the same way God treats His children it is the same way bosses treat with staff that are humble. Some bosses may be extremely difficult and may take a time to recognize the value of having a humble employee, but, as the night follows the day, whether saved or unsaved if that boss continues to illtreat the humble, God will see to the matter. God remains the justifier of all men.

In Luke 14:7-11, KJV, a parable is related by Jesus to His hearers. He spoke of what to do when we are invited to a feast. That we should

not seek to sit in the seat of honor lest someone more honourable comes, and you are humil-
iated because you have to give up your seat. He
stated that it is best to take the lower seat and
be told to come higher. These days persons want
to ensure that they are well known and so they
try to strategically position themselves among
the 'right people and be at all the right places.'
The aim is to ensure that the 'Who's who' notices
them. For a believer this is the opposite of what
is required of us. We are guaranteed promotions
when humility coupled with diligence is applied
to any assignment given.

HUMILITY IN THE HOME

Humility among members of any home is
a recipe for more peaceful days. Remember, to
be humble does not mean quiet and unassum-
ing. When a family has this virtue, it enables the
smoother flow of a lot of things. It makes love flow
easy, there is a willingness to sacrifice, there will
be hearts that will give and are compassionate.

When the husband is humble and the wife
is not, there tends to be disorder in the home as
the woman tends to speak like the authority over
the home if the husband in his humility does

not insist on the order he desires. When the wife is humble and the husband is not, there often tends to be misuse of power that can manifest in a variety of abuses, physical, emotional etc. When neither are humble, there is often competition, or they work well together but in a negative way.

Raising children that are humble is a joy. They make parenting a lot easier than the rebellious, haughty, and stiff-necked child. Though a humble child is a gem, it is not common for children to be born with a humble disposition. Parents and other forms of socialization have quite a bit to do with a child becoming humble. With the world that we are living in where everybody wants to speak loud so that their voice is heard, very few people are listening so as to appropriately respond to the different things that are being said. Women's Lib rose and whereas women were seeking a voice, in some sectors they went too far and have silenced and emasculated several of our men. More and more men are content to let the woman hunt the food and they stay home and be kept. This adjustment in our modus operandi has caused our men to soften and pushed our women to become hardened. Now you have more women that are physically and emotionally abusing their husbands or lovers. Humility in an atmosphere facilitates the serving of others.

HUMILITY IN LEADERSHIP

Nebuchadnezzar is one of the most dramatic demonstration of the self-destructive nature of not possessing humility while in a leadership position. When a President, Prime Minister, Boss, or Supervisor is prideful or narcissistic in nature, they are usually driven by the kingdom of darkness and will reject good and wise counsel as they are not conscious that they are fulfilling the agenda of the kingdom of darkness. When a leader is not humble, they cause continuous offences and are often unapologetic about their actions and are insensitive to the feelings of those that are within their care. Under such leadership people often suffer emotionally and some persons end up becoming rebellious as they do not know how to appropriately respond to this kind of oppression that they feel within themselves.

Such kind of leadership will make comfortable those like themselves and often reject those that will cause them to be introspective and take responsibility for the treatment of those in their leadership. Leaders that lack humility often also make several excuses and some may go as far as to fabricate things in an effort to ensure they are seen in a particular light by those that serve them. All these things mask the true condition of the heart and overtime can make it so impenetrable that no good or sensible or Godly inspired word can penetrate it.

BENEFITS OF HUMILITY

❖ Riches, Honour, Life

The Bible says in John 10: 10 (AMP)

> *The thief comes only in order to
> steal and kill and destroy. I came
> that they may have and enjoy life,
> and have it in abundance (to the
> full, till it overflows).*

Christ came to show us the path to life and more abundant life. Meaning, He being the Way has instructions and principles for us to be able to obtain that overflowing life. One way is through the path of humility.

Proverbs 22:4 (AMP) says:

> *The reward of humility and the
> reverent and worshipful fear of*

the Lord is riches and honor and
life.

This scripture declares that if we are humble and fear the Lord then riches, honor and life will be our just reward. And if you know the Master, He honors His words above His name and He will be a debtor to no man so if you have chosen the way of humility, you can be confident in this lifetime of these rewards!

Another scripture that shows the benefits of cultivating a humble spirit is Proverbs 15:33, KJV, which says:

The fear of the Lord is the instruc-
tion of wisdom; and before hon-
our is humility.

If a believer is to be honored by the Almighty, The Most High God, he has to be found in the way of humility, a position of servitude, having a modest opinion of himself and esteeming others higher. Humility is the low road that will guarantee you experiencing the high ways of God!

Other references: Proverbs 29:23, 18:12 (KJV)

❖ It Attracts God's Attention—Ps. 9:11-12,
   10:17 (KJV),

Psalm 9:11-12 (AMPC)

> *11 Sing praises to the Lord who
> dwells in Zion! Declare among the
> peoples His doings!*

> *12 For He Who avenges the blood
> [of His people shed unjustly]
> remembers them; He does not
> forget the cry of the afflicted (the
> poor and the humble).*

Psalm 10:17 (AMPC)

> *17 O Lord, You have heard the
> desire and the longing of the hum-
> ble and oppressed; You will pre-
> pare and strengthen and direct
> their hearts, You will cause Your
> ear to hear, 18 To do justice to the
> fatherless and the oppressed,
> so that man, who is of the earth,
> may not terrify them anymore.*

God's ears are always open to the cry of the Humble.

- ❖ Cause God to move in your favor/defer judgment 1Kings 21, KJV, 2 Kings 22:19-20, KJV, 2 Chron 12:1-8, 32:24-26, 33:11-13, KJV, Matt. 15:22-28, KJV.

  All these accounts either show how God deferred judgement, altered His very decree and brought people into mercy and favor. Lives were spared continually throughout scripture when God saw humility.

- ❖ Promotion—Job 22:29, KJV, James 4:10, KJV, 1 Peter 5:6, KJV.

Job 22:29 (AMPC)

> 29 *When they make [you] low, you will say, [There is] a lifting up; and the humble person He lifts up and saves.*

James 4:10 (AMPC)

> [10] Humble yourselves [feeling very insignificant] in the presence of the Lord, and He will exalt you [He will lift you up and make your lives significant].

1 Peter 5:6 (AMP)

> [6] Therefore humble yourselves under the mighty hand of God [set aside self-righteous pride], so that He may exalt you [to a place of honor in His service] at the appropriate time,

Other reference: Luke 14:11(KJV)

This promotion is not confined to levels and dimensions in God, but also attends to the maturing in the usage of gifts and growth and development in God in general. Immaturity in the usage of gifts is terrible. It would be like giving a state-of-the-art car to a five-year-old to drive! They will either only play with gadgets and not drive, or if they get the car to drive, they will not be skilled in maneuvering so they will wreck it and wreck themselves and possibly others. Therefore, we have to trust God's timing for exaltation.

❖ Increases grace-James 4:6 (KJV), 1 Peter 5:5 (KJV)

[12]Grace—Helps Word Studies

Cognate: 5485 *xáris* (another feminine noun from *xar-*, "*favor, disposed to, inclined, favor*able towards, *leaning towards* to share benefit")— properly, *grace*. 5485 (*xáris*) is preeminently used of the Lord's *favor—*freely *extended to give Himself* away to people (because He is "always leaning toward them").

5485 /*xáris* ("grace") answers directly to the Hebrew (OT) term 2580 /*Kaná* ("grace, *extension-toward*"). Both refer to God *freely extending* Himself (*His favor*, grace), *reaching* (*inclining*) to people because He is *disposed* to bless (be near) them.

When God increases grace, it means He leans towards you to share the benefits of HIS PRESENCE and all it represents. That will not just increase the blessings and favor, but when God leans in, it means all the enablement necessary to accomplish any task will also be accessi-

---

[12] (Biblehub.com n.d.)

ble! This means *SUPERNATURAL ENDOWMENTS,
POWER AND EXPERIENCES!*

1 Peter 5:5 (AMPC)

> [5] *Likewise, you who are younger
> and of lesser rank, be subject to
> the elders (the ministers and spiri-
> tual guides of the church)—[giving
> them due respect and yielding to
> their counsel]. Clothe (apron) your-
> selves, all of you, with humility
> [as the garb of a servant, [a]so that
> its covering cannot possibly be
> stripped from you, with freedom
> from pride and arrogance] toward
> one another. For God sets Himself
> against the proud (the insolent,
> the overbearing, the disdainful,
> the presumptuous, the boastful)—
> [and He opposes, frustrates, and
> defeats them], but gives grace
> (favor, blessing) to the humble.*

James 4:6 (AMP)

> [6] *But He gives us more and more
> grace ([a]power of the Holy Spirit,*

to meet this evil tendency and all others fully). That is why He says, God sets Himself against the proud and haughty, but gives grace [continually] to the lowly (those who are humble enough to receive it).

❖ Dwells with the humble—Isaiah 57:15 (KJV)

This dwelling of the Holy and Exalted One is not pointless. His intent is to revive (to make alive again, comfort, encourage) the spirit of the Humble.

Isaiah 57:15 (AMP)

[15] For the high and exalted One, He who inhabits eternity, Whose name is Holy says this, "I dwell on the high and holy place, But also with the [g]contrite and humble in spirit In order to revive the spirit of the humble, And to revive the heart of the contrite [overcome with sorrow for sin].

CULTIVATING HUMILITY

Romans 7:18 (KJV)

> [18] For I know that in me (that is, in my flesh,) dwelleth no good thing: for to will is present with me; but how to perform that which is good I find not.

Romans 8:13 (AMPC)

> For if you live according to [the dictates of] the flesh, you will surely die. But if through the power of the [Holy] Spirit you are [habitually] putting to death (making extinct, deadening) the [evil] deeds prompted by the body, you shall [really and genuinely] live forever.

1 John 2:16 (KJV)

> *For all that is in the world, the lust of the flesh, and the lust of the eyes, and the **pride** of **life**, is not of the Father, but is of the world.*

James 4:4 (AMPC)

> *You [are like] unfaithful wives [having illicit love affairs with the world and breaking your marriage vow to God]! Do you not know that being the world's friend is being God's enemy? So whoever chooses to be a friend of the world takes his stand as an enemy of God.*

The above scriptures point out our dilemmas and also points to the solution to the dilemmas. The Apostle Paul in a powerful discourse about him wanting to do good but struggling to do it because of a constant battle with his flesh, points out that no good thing dwells in the flesh. This concept is further backed up by what the Psalmist David said, "5 Behold, I was shapen in iniquity; and in sin did my mother conceive me" (Psalm 51:5, KJV). There is a natural proclivity towards certain sins according to our environment, bloodline and simply being human.

No one has to teach a baby how to lie, it came with their birth package. So, humility in its purest form is not natural to mankind and so if there is a little it must be harnessed and if there is none it has to be cultivated. The solution given in scripture for the issues with our flesh is to kill it! We have to fight aggressively against pride and all that is associated with it. It is a deliberate effort. The King James Version uses the word mortify. According to the [13] *Strong's Concordance*, the Greek word is thanatoóa which in this verse means to make to die i.e., destroy, render extinct (something vigorous). We are not to pet and pamper our flesh (our unholy desires or our carnal nature) but ensure we put the necessary measures in place to put it under subjection. One of the beautiful things about God, is that He provides His Spirit as an aid for our mortifying process. Thank You Jesus!

The second dilemma is the world or the world system. From the Thayer's Greek Lexicon, we learn the Greek word for world "Kosmos" means:—"worldly affairs; the aggregate of things

---

[13] (Biblehub.com 2004-2021)

earthly; the whole circle of earthly goods, endowments, riches, advantages, pleasures, etc., which, although hollow and frail and fleeting, stir desire, seduce from God and are obstacles to the cause of Christ." We therefore must maintain set standards where the world is concerned as that which is within it is geared at seducing us away from God. The statement in James 4 comes across extraordinarily strong and is to be taken with the measure with which it was intended to communicate. To be a friend of the world is to become God's enemy. God sees it as us being unfaithful wives and we know He is a very jealous Husband. To become God's enemy means a lot of hardships and oppressions in this world but the greatest lost is the permanent separation from him in hell. Knowing these things should really sober us up and help us understand the kind of Husband and Businessman God is. He is always expecting returns on every one of His investments, we are His investments, *what are your returns like lately?!*

Actions that help to cultivate humility:

- ✓ *Focus on Christ as your example.*
- ✓ *Know the greatness of your sin and the greatness of your God.*

- ✓ *Think of yourself less.*
- ✓ *Learn to give up self-defense.*
- ✓ *Be harsher on yourself than others.*
- ✓ *Never get to the place where you consider yourself humble.*
- ✓ *Be a servant to others. Mat. 20:20-29, KJV.*
- ✓ *Practice humility in the little things*
- ✓ *Delight in the Lord—not in human distinctions and accomplishments. Jer. 9:23-24, KJV.*
- ✓ *Show respect to those you do not agree with.*
- ✓ *Pursue honorable acts.*
- ✓ *A disciplined life of fasting*
- ✓ *Tithe*

All these things of course are to be done from a sincere heart with a genuine desire to be more Christlike!

A PRAYER FOR HUMILITY

Father, in the name of Jesus, I come to You seeking your help.

Wash me, O God, thoroughly with Your blood in the name of Jesus.

My Lord I pray that You will examine my heart now and purge it of everything prideful in the name of Jesus.

I want a pure heart, O God.

Please teach me how to humble myself under Your Mighty hand.

Cause me never to allow the praises of men to cause me to elevate myself in Your eyes.

Help me not to allow the blessings, opportunities, encounters nor accolades to cause me to become lifted up within myself in the name of Jesus.

I want to be numbered among the humble because they have a goodly heritage.

God, I lean on you, my expectation O God is not of mortal man but of an Eternal God.

I trust you to keep me from falling that I may be presented faultless before the presence of Your Glory in Jesus' name.

Preserve me, O God, for the sake of Your kingdom.

Give me not over to the will of man for I trust in You.

Lord, I make myself available to You,

Anoint me afresh, saturate me with your presence that I may be a good representative of You in the earth in Jesus' name.

Amen

SUMMARY

Humility as a virtue is a major theme of both the Old and New Testaments. A demeanor of humility is exactly what is needed to live in peace and harmony with all persons. By humility we cool the angry passions of others and heal old wounds. By humility we can turn enemies into friends. Humility allows us to see the dignity and worth of all God's people. Humility distinguishes the wise leader from the arrogant power-seeker. Humility releases the power of God in a situation to act quickly on someone's behalf. Humility towards elders and leaders pushes the judgement of God to be enforced against a domineering leader and from a humble leader, a release of wisdom and blessings. The spirit of humility helps us to give to ourselves the right amount of honor to self, man, and God!

Acting with humility does not in any way deny our own self-worth. Rather, it affirms the inherent worth of all persons. Wealth, power, or status gained at the expense of others brings only anxiety—never peace and love.

Note well in Isaiah 66:2b AMPC, it says, "But this is the man to whom I will look and have regard: he who is humble and of a broken or wounded spirit, and who trembles at My word and reveres My commands." One of the virtues within the persons that God will have regard for or esteem or choose to honour are those that are humble!"

The beauty about humility is that it attracts God's attention continually, and Him being a God that loves to lavish His children with an assortment of good gifts, and will trust with power, will do so bountifully!

BIBLIOGRAPHY

"Humble." In *Dictionary.com*. Lexicon LLC, n.d.

"Humility." In *Dictionary.com*. Lexicon LLC, n.d.

2004-2021. *Biblehub.com*. Accessed March 20, 2021. https://biblehub.com/hebrew/6038.htm.

2004-20021. *Biblehub.com*. Accessed March 20, 2021. https://biblehub.com/lexicon/colossians/2-18.htm.

2004-2021. *Biblehub.com*. Accessed March 18, 2021. https://biblehub.com/greek/1463.htm.

2004-2021. *Biblehub.com*. Accessed May 18, 2018. https://biblehub.com/lexicon/romans/8-13.htm.

n.d. *Biblehub.com*. Accessed January 10, 2020. https://biblehub.com/greek/5485.htm.

n.d. *BibleHub.com*. Accessed January 10, 2020. https://biblehub.com/greek/5485.htm.

Casey, Paul. n.d. *Paulcasey.org*. Accessed May 2019. https://www.paulcasey.org/the-essential-3-cs-of-vision/.

n.d. *Dictionary.com*. Accessed January 10, 2020. https://www.dictionary.com/browse/pride.

Dowgiewicz, Mike and Sue. 2005. *Restoration Ministries*. Accessed July 5, 2018. file:///C:/Users/nicho/Downloads/DemolishingStrongholds[1].pdf.

Guzik, David. 2018. *Enduringword.com*. Accessed May 2019. https://enduringword.com/bible-commentary/joshua-9/.

Smith, William. 2019. *Biblestudytools.com*. AccessedMay2019.https://www.biblestudy-tools.com/dictionary/nebuchadnezzar/.

"Humilty". Quotes. Accessed March 20, 2018, https://www.brainyquote.com/search_results?q=humility#

Joyner, Rick. *The Final Quest*. Fort Mill, SC: MorningStar Publications, 2010.

"Strong's Concordance". Lexicon. Accessed March 12, 2018, https://biblehub.com/greek/1463.htm

"Helps-Word Studies". Lexicon. Accessed March 12, 2018, https://biblehub.com/greek/1463.htm

"Strong's Exhaustive Concordance". Lexicon. Accessed March 12, 2018, https://biblehub. com/greek/1463.htm

"Thayer's Greek Lexicon". Lexicon. Accessed March 12, 2018, https://biblehub.com/ greek/1463.htm

"Thayer's Greek Lexicon. Lexicon. Accessed May 18, 2018https://biblehub.com/lexicon/ romans/8-13.htm

"Ellicott's Commentary for English Readers." Bible Commentaries. Accessed March 21, 2021. https://biblehub.com/commentaries/.

"Ellicott's Commentary for English Readers." Bible Commentaries. Accessed March 21, 2021. https://biblehub.com/commentaries/, Paragraph 3.

"BibleGateway." BibleGateway.com. 1 Peter 5:5. Accessed March 21, 2021. https://classic. biblegateway.com/about/.

"BibleGateway," BibleGateway.com (1 Peter 5:5), accessed March 21, 2021, https://classic. biblegateway.com/about/.

9 781637 693544